HOW TO SELL ON TIKTOK FOR FASHION BRANDS

Mastering Viral Marketing With
Trendy Tactics For Your Fashion Line

By

Genevieve Allan

Table of Contents

Chapter 1

Understanding TikTok and Its Audience

Welcome to the exciting realm of TikTok, the social media platform that has rapidly become a global sensation. For those in the fashion sector aiming to leverage this platform, it's important to grasp the essence of TikTok and its audience.

TikTok is a platform designed for short videos, ranging from 15 seconds to three minutes. What sets TikTok apart is its potential for making any user go viral. Its algorithm doesn't just support well-known influencers; it offers everyone an equal opportunity to gain visibility. This results in a vibrant and thrilling space where creativity thrives.

The user demographic on TikTok is broad, but it tends to be younger. Most users are aged between 16 and 24, making it a hub for youth culture and trends. This demographic has a keen interest in fashion, making TikTok an ideal venue for fashion brands aiming to connect with a younger, trend-conscious audience. Knowing this demographic is crucial for developing content that hits the mark.

TikTok's culture is fast-moving and constantly evolving. Trends can appear and disappear quickly, making it vital for brands to remain flexible and trend-aware. Engaging with these trends can help your brand gain attention. However, it's not just about jumping on trends; it's about bringing your unique perspective to them.

Engagement is a significant aspect of TikTok. Users are not just passive observers; they actively interact by liking, commenting, and sharing. This high level of interaction means that creating content that encourages user participation can greatly increase your reach.

Inviting users to take part in challenges or use branded hashtags can create a viral effect, spreading your brand's message widely.

Case studies of successful fashion brands on TikTok reveal a common factor: authenticity. Users value brands that come across as genuine and relatable. The polished, perfect images that are common on other social media platforms don't perform as well here. Instead, behind-the-scenes glimpses, raw footage, and authentic moments capture the audience's attention. Displaying the human side of your brand can foster trust and loyalty.

TikTok also offers a variety of features to enhance your content. From music and sound effects to filters and special effects, these tools can make your videos more engaging and fun. Utilizing these features can help your brand stand out in the competitive TikTok environment.

As we delve further into this chapter, we'll explore these aspects in greater detail. You'll learn how to identify and understand your target audience, analyze user behavior, and strategically position your brand on TikTok. By the end of this chapter, you'll have a comprehensive understanding of what drives TikTok and how you can harness it to elevate your fashion brand.

So, let's embark on this thrilling journey. Grasping TikTok and its audience is the initial step towards mastering this influential platform and unlocking its full potential for your fashion brand. Prepare to embrace the creativity, spontaneity, and vibrancy that characterize TikTok, and discover how it can revolutionize your social media marketing approach.

Introduction to TikTok

TikTok has swiftly risen to become one of the most favored social media platforms globally. Since its inception in 2016, it has enabled users to create and share short videos accompanied by music, utilizing a vast array of creative tools. Unlike other social media, TikTok centers on easily consumable, short-form content that fits perfectly into the fast-paced nature of the digital age.

A striking aspect of TikTok is its focus on fun and imaginative expression. Users can enhance their videos with music, sound effects, filters, and special effects, providing limitless creative options. Whether participating in dance challenges, crafting humorous skits, or sharing fashion advice, TikTok encourages unique and captivating self-expression.

The platform's distinctive algorithm also sets it apart. The "For You" page delivers a personalized stream of videos tailored to each user's preferences, allowing even new users to gain exposure if their content strikes a chord with viewers. This environment rewards creativity and originality, making viral moments possible in a short span of time.

TikTok's user base is both diverse and lively, attracting individuals from various backgrounds. Nonetheless, it holds particular appeal for younger audiences, especially teenagers and those in their early twenties. This group is constantly seeking the latest trends, making TikTok an ideal platform for fashion brands aiming to engage with young, trend-aware consumers.

For fashion brands, TikTok presents a unique chance to display products in a manner that feels genuine and relatable. By understanding the platform's culture and leveraging its features, brands can produce content that not only entertains but also fosters engagement and boosts sales. In the upcoming sections, we will delve into strategies for effectively utilizing TikTok to enhance your fashion brand's visibility and reach.

Demographics and User Behavior

Knowing who uses TikTok is crucial for crafting content that resonates. While TikTok boasts a vast global audience, it's especially favored by younger generations. The majority of TikTok users are between 16 and 24 years old, making it particularly popular with Gen Z. This group is recognized for its digital proficiency, trendsetting habits, and a strong liking for visual content.

Gen Z has grown up immersed in technology, with smartphones and social media being integral parts of their lives. They appreciate authenticity and are more likely to engage with content that feels genuine and relatable. Thus, highly polished and overly produced videos might not perform as well as more natural, behind-the-scenes clips that reveal the human side of a brand. For fashion brands, this means highlighting the creative process, sharing day-in-the-life moments, and featuring real customers wearing their products.

Another important element of TikTok user behavior is their enthusiasm for trends. Whether it's a new dance challenge, a viral hashtag, or a trending sound, TikTok users eagerly participate in the latest crazes. This trend-focused culture requires brands to stay updated on what's popular and find ways to engage with these trends in a manner consistent with their brand identity. Creating content that aligns with these trends can significantly enhance visibility and engagement.

TikTok users are also very interactive. They don't just passively watch videos; they like, comment, share, and even create their own versions of popular content. This interactive aspect offers brands a great chance to connect directly with their audience. Encouraging user-generated content, initiating challenges, and actively responding to comments can help build a loyal community around a brand.

In summary, TikTok's audience is young, trend-conscious, and highly interactive. By understanding these demographics and behaviors, fashion brands can tailor their content to better connect with their audience, resulting in higher engagement and success on the platform.

Why TikTok Matters for Fashion Brands

TikTok has revolutionized the fashion industry by offering a highly engaging and visually appealing platform. One of the key reasons TikTok is significant is its capability to connect with a vast, global audience. With millions of active users, fashion brands can present their products to a wide and diverse group of people worldwide.

The platform's format is ideal for fashion content. Short, engaging videos enable brands to showcase their products in dynamic and innovative ways. Whether it's a quick styling tip, a behind-the-scenes look at a photoshoot, or unveiling a new collection, TikTok's video-centric nature allows fashion brands to narrate their story more effectively than static images.

TikTok's algorithm significantly enhances its value for fashion brands. Unlike other social media platforms where gaining a large audience typically requires a substantial follower base, TikTok's algorithm allows any user to potentially go viral. This provides even smaller brands the opportunity for considerable visibility if their content strikes a chord with users. For fashion brands, this means that new collections or distinctive pieces can reach millions of viewers.

The trend-focused culture of TikTok is another crucial aspect. Fashion thrives on staying ahead of trends, and TikTok is a breeding ground for many of these trends. By engaging in trending challenges and using popular sounds, fashion brands can place themselves at the cutting edge of what's new and exciting. This not only increases brand visibility but also associates the brand with current cultural trends.

Additionally, TikTok's interactive user base allows brands to build deeper connections with their audience. Inviting users to participate in challenges, use branded hashtags, or create content featuring their products can foster a strong sense of community and loyalty.

In summary, TikTok provides fashion brands with a unique platform to creatively display their products, engage with a global audience, and stay ahead of trends. It's a space where authenticity and creativity are valued, making it an essential tool for any fashion brand aiming to make a significant impact.

Case Studies: Successful Fashion Brands on TikTok

Observing the success of fashion brands on TikTok offers valuable lessons on effective strategies. One notable example is Guess. Early in TikTok's rise, Guess initiated the #InMyDenim challenge, encouraging users to share their transformation from casual outfits to stylish denim looks. This challenge went viral, amassing millions of views and significantly enhancing the brand's visibility on the platform.

Gymshark, known for its fitness apparel, excels at creating engaging, fitness-related content. They frequently partner with fitness influencers who showcase their products in workout routines, producing content that is both motivational and closely aligned with their brand. This strategy not only promotes their products but also fosters a community of fitness enthusiasts around their brand.

Fashion Nova, a fast-fashion retailer, has also achieved remarkable success on TikTok. They regularly post videos featuring influencers and everyday users wearing their clothes in various settings. By sharing user-generated content, Fashion Nova keeps their feed relatable and dynamic. This approach has helped them build a large following and cultivate a sense of community among their customers.

Aritzia, a women's fashion brand, takes a different route by focusing on high-quality, aesthetically pleasing content that appeals to their target audience. They use TikTok to creatively showcase their latest collections, often incorporating popular sounds and trends. Their polished and trendy videos resonate with their fashion-forward audience, enhancing their brand image and engagement.

These brands have succeeded by understanding TikTok's audience and tailoring their content to fit. They capitalize on trends, collaborate with influencers, and encourage user participation while maintaining a strong brand identity. These case studies illustrate that with the right approach, fashion brands can effectively use TikTok to increase their visibility, connect with their audience, and drive sales. Analyzing these examples can provide inspiration and strategies to enhance your own TikTok marketing efforts.

Chapter 2

Crafting Your Brand's TikTok Strategy

Now that we've covered the fundamentals of TikTok and examined successful examples, it's time to delve into crafting your own brand strategy. Developing an effective TikTok strategy goes beyond merely posting videos; it requires thoughtful planning, creativity, and a deep understanding of your brand's distinctive voice and objectives.

Firstly, setting clear goals is crucial. What do you aim to accomplish on TikTok? Are you focused on enhancing brand awareness, driving website traffic, or increasing sales? Clearly defined goals will actually guide your content creation and also overall strategy. Without specific objectives, it's easy to become lost amid the platform's constant stream of trends and content.

Next, identifying your target audience is essential. Understanding whom you want to reach will shape the type of content you produce. TikTok's audience is diverse, so pinpointing a specific demographic can enhance the effectiveness of your efforts. Consider factors such as age, interests, and behaviors when defining your audience, enabling you to create content that resonates and engages your desired viewers.

Analyzing competitors can also offer valuable insights. Study the strategies of other fashion brands on TikTok, particularly those that have achieved success. What types of content do they share? How do they interact with their audience? Learning from their approaches can help you avoid common pitfalls and uncover new opportunities.

Consistency plays a pivotal role on TikTok. Developing a content calendar can help you stay organized and ensure a steady flow of posts. Regular updates keep your audience engaged and maintain visibility. However, it's not just about frequency; the quality and creativity of your content are equally important.

Lastly, embrace experimentation. TikTok rewards creativity and originality. Test different formats, participate in trending challenges, and listen to feedback from your audience. Remaining adaptable and open to new concepts will keep your content dynamic and pertinent.

In this chapter, we'll delve deeply into these aspects, equipping you with the strategies and tools needed to craft a TikTok strategy that enhances your fashion brand. Let's embark on creating a plan that captures attention and delivers significant outcomes.

Setting Clear Objectives and Goals

Before you start creating content for TikTok, it's essential to set clear objectives and goals for your brand. These goals will act as your roadmap, guiding your strategy and helping you measure your success on the platform.

Begin by determining what you want to achieve with TikTok. Are you looking to raise brand awareness among younger audiences? Do you aim to drive traffic to your online store or generate leads for your latest fashion line? By setting specific, measurable goals, such as reaching a certain number of followers, increasing engagement rates, or hitting a conversion target, you can tailor your content and tactics to meet these objectives.

Make sure your TikTok goals align with your overall marketing and business objectives. Your strategy on TikTok should complement your broader brand strategy, reinforcing your brand message and values. For instance, if sustainability is a core value of your brand, your TikTok content could highlight eco-friendly fashion tips or showcase your ethical production processes.

Also, think about the timeline for reaching your goals. Are you focusing on short-term achievements, such as launching a new product campaign, or are you looking at long-term brand building? Setting realistic timelines helps you stay accountable and allows for adjustments based on performance insights gathered from TikTok analytics.

Be prepared to adjust and refine your goals as you gain more experience on TikTok. The platform's dynamic nature means that trends and audience preferences can change quickly. Being adaptable and ready to pivot your strategy based on data-driven insights will help you stay ahead of trends and maintain relevance in the fast-paced world of social media.

By establishing clear objectives and goals for your TikTok strategy, you create a solid foundation for producing content that resonates with your audience and achieves meaningful results for your fashion brand. In the upcoming sections, we'll discuss how to turn these goals into actionable steps and effective content strategies.

Identifying Your Target Audience

Grasping your target audience is key to producing engaging content on TikTok. Start by outlining demographic details such as age, gender, location, and income level that match your fashion brand's offerings. For example, if your brand focuses on trendy streetwear, your target market might consist of younger, city-dwelling individuals with an interest in fashion-forward styles.

In addition to demographics, think about psychographic factors like interests, values, and lifestyle choices. Are your potential customers environmentally aware, driven by luxury, or fitness enthusiasts? Recognizing these aspects helps you create content that aligns with their interests and values, establishing a stronger connection.

Analyzing your current customer base can also provide useful insights into your potential TikTok audience. Examine data from other social media platforms, customer surveys, and website analytics to identify trends and preferences. This information can inform your content strategy and messaging to better engage your target audience on TikTok.

Also, observe audience behaviors on TikTok. What types of content actually do they interact with? Which hashtags and trends are they following? By immersing yourself in the TikTok community and monitoring user interactions, you can better understand what grabs their attention and encourages engagement.

Creating distinct audience personas can further refine your targeting. Develop fictional profiles of your ideal customers based on shared traits and behaviors. This approach allows you to personalize your content and messaging to address specific needs and interests, enhancing relevance and connection with your audience.

Identifying your target audience involves a mix of demographic, psychographic, and behavioral insights. By understanding who your audience is and what motivates them, you can create TikTok content that speaks directly to their preferences and drives meaningful engagement for your fashion brand.

Analyzing Competitors

Analyzing your competitors on TikTok offers valuable insights into successful strategies within your industry and can inspire new ideas for your content strategy. Begin by pinpointing key competitors, including other fashion brands or influencers who share a similar target audience and are active on TikTok.

Observe the type of content they produce. Do they emphasize product showcases, behind-the-scenes glimpses, or user-generated content? Notice their tone, visual style, and branding consistency. Understanding these aspects can help you distinguish your brand and find unique ways to engage your audience.

Pay attention to their engagement metrics, such as likes, comments, and shares. High engagement rates suggest content that resonates with their audience, providing hints about what might work for yours.

Examine their use of TikTok features, including trending sounds, effects, and challenges. Are they participating in viral trends or creating their own? Analyzing how competitors use these features can give you ideas for your own content and help you stay up-to-date with TikTok's changing trends.

Also, track their follower growth and audience interactions over time. Are they gaining followers steadily, or do they experience spikes during certain campaigns or content releases? Understanding their growth patterns can inform your own strategies and help you predict market shifts.

The purpose of analyzing competitors on TikTok is not to copy them but to innovate. By learning from their successes and identifying gaps or opportunities, you can refine your TikTok strategy to better position your fashion brand and effectively attract and engage your target audience.

Aligning TikTok Strategy with Overall Brand Strategy

Integrating your TikTok strategy with your broader brand strategy is crucial for maintaining consistency and reinforcing your brand identity across all platforms. Start by revisiting your brand's core values and unique selling points. These should form the basis of your TikTok content, showcasing what distinguishes your fashion brand from competitors.

Consider how your brand voice translates onto TikTok. Whether it's playful, inspirational, or informative, maintaining a consistent tone helps build brand recognition and authenticity. Aligning your TikTok content with your brand's established voice and values strengthens connections with your audience, emphasizing why they should engage with your brand.

Additionally, ensure that your TikTok content aligns with your overall marketing objectives. Whether your goal is to increase brand awareness, drive traffic to your website, or boost sales, each piece of content should contribute to these goals. This alignment ensures that your TikTok efforts are not just creative but also strategically impactful, maximizing their effectiveness within your broader marketing strategy.

Visual coherence is also essential. Your TikTok videos should reflect your brand's aesthetic and visual identity. Consistency in color schemes and editing styles reinforces brand recognition and enhances the professional appeal of your content.

Finally, adapt your TikTok strategy to complement other marketing channels. Consider how TikTok can integrate with platforms like Instagram, Facebook, or your website. By cross-promoting content and maintaining a consistent message across channels, you enhance brand visibility and encourage audience engagement across multiple touchpoints.

Aligning your TikTok strategy with your overall brand strategy creates a cohesive brand experience that resonates with your audience and strengthens your position in the competitive fashion industry. This unified approach not only enhances brand consistency but also fosters meaningful connections and long-term loyalty among your customers.

Chapter 3

Creating Engaging Content

Creating engaging content is central to a successful TikTok strategy. This chapter will guide you through crafting videos that capture attention, drive interaction, and showcase your brand's personality.

TikTok is all about creativity and authenticity. Unlike other platforms, TikTok users value raw, unfiltered content that feels genuine. This means you don't need a big budget or fancy equipment to make an impact. Instead, focus on storytelling and being real. Whether it's a behind-the-scenes look at your design process or a candid moment with your team, showing the authentic side of your brand can create a stronger connection with viewers.

Figuring out what type of content works best for your brand is essential. Are your followers interested in styling tips, DIY fashion hacks, or the latest trends? Experiment well with different formats actually to see what resonates. Don't hesitate to try new things—TikTok thrives on spontaneity and experimentation. The more you explore, the better you'll understand what clicks with your audience.

Music and trends are significant on TikTok. Using popular sounds and joining viral challenges can help your content reach a wider audience. Keep up with the latest trends and think about how you can creatively incorporate them into your videos while staying true to your brand.

Engagement is vital on TikTok. Encourage your followers to interact with your content by asking questions, running challenges, or using interactive features like polls and duets. The more you engage with your audience, the more likely they are to engage back, increasing your visibility on the platform.

In this chapter, we'll explore these strategies in more detail, offering tips and examples to help you create content that not only entertains but also drives meaningful engagement for your fashion brand. Get ready to unleash your creativity and make a lasting impression on TikTok.

Types of Content That Perform Well

Creating content that connects with your audience is crucial for success on TikTok. Although the platform thrives on creativity, certain types of content consistently perform well and can enhance your brand's visibility.

1. Challenges and Trends: Joining popular challenges and trends is an excellent way to increase your

content's reach. Whether it's a dance challenge or a viral hashtag, participating shows that your brand is up-to-date with current trends. Add your unique twist to actually make your content stand out.

2. Behind-the-Scenes: Viewers enjoy seeing the process behind their favorite products. Sharing behind-the-scenes footage of your fashion pieces being designed, produced, or styled can foster a deeper connection with your audience. It humanizes your brand and offers followers a glimpse into your creative process.

3. Styling Tips and Tutorials: Educational content like styling tips and tutorials is highly appreciated. Show your audience different ways to wear your pieces or provide advice on fashion trends. This type of content positions your brand as an expert and offers practical value to your viewers.

4. User-Generated Content: Encourage your customers to actually create content featuring your products. Sharing user-generated content provides social proof and helps build a community around

your brand. It shows that real people love and use your products, making them more relatable to potential customers.

5. Collaborations with Influencers: Partnering with influencers can significantly expand your reach. Influencers bring their own audience and credibility, introducing your brand to new followers. Choose influencers whose style aligns with your brand for optimal results.

6. Product Launches and Announcements: Use TikTok to create excitement around new product launches or significant announcements. Teasers, countdowns, and reveal videos can generate anticipation among your followers.

7. Entertaining Content: TikTok is fundamentally about entertainment. Fun, humorous, or visually appealing content can captivate viewers and encourage shares. Don't hesitate to show the lighter side of your brand and have fun with your content.

By experimenting with these content types, you can determine what works best for your brand and audience. The key is to remain authentic, be creative, and continuously experiment to see what resonates most with your followers.

The Art of Storytelling in Fashion

Storytelling is an essential element in fashion marketing, as it helps create a deeper emotional connection with your audience. It goes beyond simply displaying your products, transforming your brand into something memorable and meaningful.

Begin by reflecting on your brand's origins. Why was it created? What drives your designs? Sharing your journey, values, and inspirations crafts a relatable narrative for your audience. People tend to connect more with a brand that has a compelling story rather than one that solely focuses on selling products.

Each collection or individual piece can have its own story as well. What sparked the designs for this season? Is there a specific theme or message you want to express? For instance, if your latest collection draws from vintage fashion, discuss the history and nostalgia that influenced your creations. This adds layers to your products, giving your audience something relatable and exciting.

Storytelling involves more than words; visuals are equally important. Use high-quality images and videos to illustrate your story. Display your products in various settings, narrate their creation process, and highlight their unique features. Behind-the-scenes content can be particularly engaging, offering a glimpse into your creative process.

Incorporate your customers' stories as well. User-generated content and testimonials bring authenticity to your narrative. Featuring real people wearing your products and sharing their experiences fosters a sense of community and trust around your brand.

Above all, maintain authenticity. Genuine storytelling builds trust and loyalty. Don't shy away from revealing the human side of your brand, including the ups and downs. Your audience will value the honesty and realness, increasing the likelihood of them becoming loyal customers.

Integrating storytelling into your TikTok strategy can help your brand stand out in a competitive market. It's about forging connections, evoking emotions, and making your audience feel like they are part of your brand's journey.

Leveraging TikTok's Features: Music, Effects, and Trends

TikTok stands out from other social platforms due to its distinctive features. To maximize your TikTok presence, it's crucial to understand how to utilize music, effects, and trends effectively.

Music

Music plays a central role on TikTok. Incorporating trending songs or sounds can significantly enhance your content's visibility. Stay updated on popular tracks within the app and consider their relevance to your videos. Whether it's a lively backdrop for a fashion showcase or a tune that reflects your brand's vibe, choosing the right music can make your content more appealing and relatable. TikTok offers a vast selection of licensed music, making it easy to find tracks that align with your brand's identity.

Effects

TikTok provides a wide array of effects to add creativity to your videos. From visual filters that enhance aesthetics to interactive effects that respond to gestures, these tools can elevate your content. Experiment with different effects to discover what complements your brand best. For example, applying a specific filter that matches your clothing line's style can maintain a cohesive look across your videos. Embrace new effects as they are introduced; staying current with TikTok's features demonstrates your brand's flexibility and innovation.

Trends

Trends are pivotal on TikTok. Participating in popular challenges, memes, or hashtag trends can expand your content's reach. Monitor trending topics on the platform and brainstorm ways to incorporate them into your videos while staying authentic to your brand. For instance, if there's a trending dance challenge, consider featuring your team or influencers performing it in your latest collection. This not only keeps your content relevant but also engaging and enjoyable for viewers.

By effectively harnessing music, effects, and trends, you can craft dynamic and captivating TikTok content that resonates with your audience. These features empower you to showcase your brand's creativity and maintain fresh, stimulating content. Embrace TikTok's unique tools to enrich your videos and forge deeper connections with your audience in innovative ways.

Content Calendar and Consistency

Developing a content calendar and maintaining regularity are vital for achieving success on TikTok. Consistent posting not only keeps your audience engaged but also strengthens your brand's visibility on the platform.

Content Calendar

A content calendar serves as a planning tool to organize and schedule posts in advance. Begin by determining your posting frequency. While there's no universal rule, aiming for several posts per week can sustain visibility. Structure your content around themes or campaigns; designate specific days for behind-the-scenes insights, styling tips, or user-generated content. This approach not only enhances organization but also ensures a diverse array of content to sustain audience interest.

Utilize the calendar to plan for upcoming events, holidays, or product launches. By scheduling posts ahead of time, you can create timely and pertinent content without last-minute pressure. This strategy also allows flexibility to integrate emerging TikTok trends into your scheduled content.

Consistency

Consistency plays a pivotal role in cultivating a dedicated TikTok following. Regular posting maintains your brand's prominence in followers' minds. Beyond frequency, maintaining a uniform brand voice and visual style reinforces brand identity and facilitates instant recognition.

Engagement is integral to consistency as well. Responding to comments, interacting with followers, and actively participating in trends demonstrate your brand's engagement within the TikTok community. These actions foster deeper connections with your audience, prompting increased interaction with your content.

Establishing and adhering to a content calendar ensures a steady posting schedule, fostering follower growth and heightened engagement over time. By staying organized and adhering to a consistent posting regimen, you can establish a robust presence on TikTok and effectively engage with your audience.

Chapter 4

Leveraging Influencers and Collaborations

In the realm of TikTok, influencers and partnerships play a significant role in expanding your brand's reach. Collaborating with the right influencers can introduce your fashion line to a wider audience, generate excitement, and bolster your brand's credibility.

Influencers are individuals who have amassed a sizable following and wield influence over their audience's opinions and actions. They range from mega-influencers with millions of followers to micro-influencers who cater to more specialized, engaged communities. Each type of influencer offers distinct advantages, depending on your campaign objectives and target demographic.

Partnering with influencers enables you to leverage their established trust and connection with their followers. An authentic endorsement from an influencer can ignite interest and interaction among their audience, which is particularly potent for fashion brands as influencers often dictate trends and influence their followers' tastes.

Selecting the right influencers is critical. Seek out influencers whose style and values resonate with your brand. Authenticity is paramount; an influencer genuinely enthusiastic about and using your products will resonate more effectively with their followers. Assess their engagement metrics and audience demographics to ensure alignment with your brand's goals.

This chapter will delve into various strategies for identifying and collaborating with influencers. It will cover approaches for initiating partnerships, negotiating terms, and crafting content that mutually benefits both parties. Furthermore, it will address methods to evaluate the success of these collaborations, ensuring they deliver a favorable return on investment.

By effectively leveraging influencers and partnerships, you can enhance your brand's visibility and establish meaningful connections with potential customers. This chapter aims to equip you with the insights and tools necessary to cultivate successful influencer relationships that drive growth and engagement for your fashion brand.

Finding the Right Influencers for Your Brand

Identifying the right influencers for your brand is crucial for forming effective partnerships that resonate with your audience. Here's how to find them:

1. Clarify Your Objectives: Begin by defining what you aim to achieve through influencer collaborations. Are you focused on increasing

brand visibility, driving sales, or promoting a new product line? Understanding your goals helps pinpoint influencers who can best support your objectives.

2. Know Your Audience: Gain insights into your target demographic's demographics, interests, and online behaviors. This knowledge guides your search for influencers whose followers closely match your customer profile. Social media analytics tools offer valuable data to identify influencers whose audience aligns with yours.

3. Research Potential Influencers: Start by exploring influencers already active in your industry or promoting similar brands. Use relevant hashtags to locate influencers whose content aligns with your brand ethos. Platforms like Instagram, YouTube, and TikTok provide search features that simplify this process.

4. Assess Engagement Metrics: While large follower counts are impressive, engagement metrics such as likes, comments, and shares indicate an

influencer's impact. Look for influencers whose audience actively engages with their posts, demonstrating genuine interest in their content.

5. Evaluate Content Quality and Style: Assess the visual appeal and production quality of an influencer's content. Does it reflect your brand's aesthetic standards? Consistent, high-quality content is pivotal for maintaining your brand's image and connecting with your audience.

6. Authenticity and Alignment: Select influencers who genuinely resonate with your brand values and can authentically endorse your products. Authenticity fosters trust and credibility, enhancing the effectiveness of their promotional efforts among followers.

7. Micro vs. Macro Influencers: Consider the scale of influence that best suits your campaign objectives. Micro-influencers (10,000 - 100,000 followers) often boast higher engagement rates and cater to niche audiences. Macro-influencers (100,000+ followers) offer broader reach but may have

slightly lower engagement rates per follower. Choose based on which aligns better with your specific goals.

By meticulously choosing influencers aligned with your brand values and objectives, you can cultivate impactful partnerships that drive engagement and business growth. This targeted approach ensures authenticity and relevance, resonating effectively with your intended audience.

Building Mutually Beneficial Relationships

Establishing effective, mutually beneficial relationships with influencers is crucial for successful collaborations. When both parties feel valued and committed, partnerships are more likely to yield excellent outcomes.

1. Open Communication: Begin with transparent and clear communication. Clearly define your campaign objectives, expectations, and the scope of work. Ensuring that influencers understand their role and what you aim to achieve helps prevent misunderstandings and aligns everyone's efforts.

2. Fair Compensation: Respect influencers' time and efforts by offering fair compensation, whether through monetary payment, product samples, or a combination. Recognizing their contribution and compensating them appropriately fosters professionalism and goodwill in the partnership.

3. Flexibility and Creative Freedom: Allow influencers creative latitude to produce content that authentically reflects their style. While guidelines are important to maintain brand alignment, overly restrictive rules can stifle creativity. Trusting influencers to connect with their audience in their own voice often leads to more engaging content.

4. Long-Term Relationships: Aim for sustained partnerships rather than one-off collaborations.

Long-term relationships allow influencers to develop deeper familiarity with your brand, resulting in more genuine and effective content. Consistent endorsement over time also builds credibility with their followers.

5. Show Appreciation: Demonstrate gratitude for influencers' contributions. Simple acts such as acknowledging their efforts, sharing their content on your platforms, and offering positive feedback contribute to a positive working relationship.

6. Provide Resources: Equip influencers with necessary resources like high-quality images, product samples, or insider insights about your brand. Better resources empower influencers to create compelling content that resonates with their audience and promotes your products effectively.

7. Measure and Share Insights: Share campaign results with influencers to illustrate the impact of their efforts. Providing performance metrics not only validates their contribution but also informs

future strategies. This collaborative feedback loop fosters ongoing improvement and mutual success.

By adhering to these principles, you can cultivate strong, mutually beneficial relationships with influencers. These partnerships enhance your brand's visibility, credibility, and foster a supportive environment where both parties can thrive and achieve shared goals.

Crafting Effective Collaboration Campaigns

Creating a successful collaboration campaign with influencers requires thorough planning and a well-defined strategy. Here are key steps to ensure your campaigns achieve impact:

1. Establish Clear Objectives: Begin by outlining specific goals for your campaign, such as boosting brand awareness, driving sales, or launching a new

product. These objectives will guide your planning and serve as benchmarks for measuring success.

2. Understand Your Audience: Identify the demographics and interests of your target audience to align with the influencer's followers. This alignment ensures your campaign reaches individuals who are likely interested in your brand, enhancing its effectiveness.

3. Select Appropriate Influencers: Choose influencers whose values, style, and audience demographics align closely with your brand. Authenticity and engagement are more important than mere follower count. A well-matched influencer can foster a genuine connection with their audience, yielding better outcomes.

4. Craft a Detailed Creative Brief: Provide influencers with a comprehensive brief outlining campaign goals, key messages, and specific content requirements. While offering guidelines, allow influencers creative freedom to ensure the

content feels genuine and resonates with their audience.

5. Develop Compelling Content: Collaborate with influencers to create engaging content that suits their followers. This may include product demonstrations, tutorials, behind-the-scenes glimpses, or lifestyle content seamlessly integrating your products without appearing overly promotional.

6. Utilize Hashtags and Challenges: Incorporate relevant hashtags and participate in TikTok challenges to expand your campaign's visibility. Engaging in trending topics can broaden your reach and encourage audience participation.

7. Implement Cross-Promotion: Extend your campaign's reach beyond TikTok by promoting content across other social media platforms, your website, and email newsletters. This multi-channel approach reinforces your message across various touchpoints.

8. Monitor and Evaluate Performance: Utilize TikTok's analytics tools to monitor key metrics such as views, likes, shares, and comments. Assess engagement levels and gather feedback to identify successful strategies and areas for improvement.

9. Conduct Post-Campaign Evaluation: Review campaign results with the influencer to analyze what worked well and gather insights for future collaborations. Building a strong rapport with influencers fosters ongoing success and mutually beneficial partnerships.

By following these steps, you can develop effective collaboration campaigns that not only elevate your brand's visibility but also resonate deeply with your target audience. This strategic approach ensures that both your brand and the influencer derive value, creating a mutually beneficial outcome.

Measuring Influencer Campaign Success

After launching an influencer campaign, it's important to assess its effectiveness to understand its impact and enhance future efforts. Here's how to accurately gauge the success of your influencer campaigns:

1. Establish Clear KPIs: Before launching, define key performance indicators (KPIs) such as reach, engagement (likes, comments, shares), website traffic, and sales. These metrics help quantify the campaign's impact on your brand.

2. Utilize Analytics Tools: Social media platforms like TikTok offer analytics tools that provide insightful data. Monitor metrics like views, likes, shares, and comments to assess the campaign's reach and audience engagement.

3. Track Sales and Traffic: Employ tools like Google Analytics to track website traffic and sales attributed to the campaign. Analyze referral sources to gauge how much traffic originated from

the influencer's posts, helping measure direct financial outcomes.

4. Monitor Engagement Rates: High engagement rates, including comments and shares, indicate content resonance. Detailed comments and active sharing reflect strong audience engagement, providing deeper insights into content reception.

5. Seek Feedback: Gather qualitative insights from influencers and their audience through comments and direct messages. This feedback offers perspectives on how the campaign was perceived and suggestions for improvement.

6. Evaluate ROI: Calculate ROI by comparing campaign costs to generated revenue. Consider direct sales and secondary benefits like heightened brand awareness and new followers. A positive ROI signifies campaign success.

7. Benchmark Comparison: Assess campaign performance against previous efforts or industry benchmarks to gauge effectiveness and identify areas for improvement.

8. Assess Long-term Impact: Monitor metrics over time to observe sustained increases in brand awareness, engagement, or sales beyond the campaign period. Influencer campaigns can have enduring effects.

9. Document Insights: After evaluation, document successful strategies and areas needing improvement. Use these learnings to refine future influencer campaigns, ensuring continuous improvement and adaptation.

By adhering to these steps, you can effectively measure the success of your influencer campaigns, leveraging data-driven insights to maximize returns and optimize your influencer marketing strategy.

Chapter 5

Analyzing Performance and Scaling Success

Once your TikTok campaigns are live, effectively evaluating their performance is crucial for continuous improvement and advancement. This chapter provides a comprehensive guide on assessing your campaigns and leveraging insights to expand your achievements.

Evaluating performance goes beyond surface metrics like likes and views. It involves delving into data to comprehend audience preferences and behaviors. This includes tracking essential metrics, interpreting outcomes, and deriving actionable insights to shape future strategies. Understanding which content resonates best and which influencers drive significant engagement enables you to refine tactics and allocate resources more efficiently.

Scaling success entails amplifying proven strategies. This may involve increasing investment in top-performing campaigns, broadening influencer collaborations, or experimenting with promising new content formats. It's about building on successes and learning from less effective endeavors to continuously refine your marketing approach.

This chapter covers the setup of effective tracking and analytics systems. It emphasizes the importance of establishing clear, measurable goals and utilizing tools such as TikTok Analytics, Google Analytics, and social media dashboards to gather and analyze data. You'll learn how to identify trends and patterns in performance metrics and translate these insights into informed decision-making.

Additionally, strategies for scaling successful campaigns are explored. This includes boosting investment in high-performing areas, exploring new growth opportunities, and remaining adaptable to platform and market shifts.

By the end of this chapter, you'll possess a solid grasp of analyzing TikTok campaign performance and scaling efforts for sustained success. This knowledge empowers you to make data-driven choices that enhance your brand's TikTok presence and foster ongoing growth.

Key Metrics to Track on TikTok

Tracking the appropriate metrics on TikTok is essential for comprehending how well your campaigns are performing and for making informed choices. Here are the key metrics you should prioritize:

1. Views: This indicates how many times your video has been watched, reflecting your content's reach. While a high view count shows broad exposure, it's crucial to examine other metrics for engagement insights.

2. Likes: The number of times viewers have appreciated your video by liking it. A higher number of likes typically indicates that your content has resonated well with your audience.

3. Comments: Comments provide valuable insights into viewer engagement. Positive and detailed comments suggest strong interaction. Engaging with comments can also foster a sense of community around your brand.

4. Shares: This metric indicates how frequently your video has been shared, signaling engagement and potential virality. Shares expand your content's reach to new audiences.

5. Follower Growth: Tracking changes in your follower count over time indicates how effective

your content strategy is in attracting new followers.

6. Engagement Rate: Combining likes, comments, and shares relative to views offers a comprehensive view of your content's engagement level. Higher engagement rates indicate active interaction with your content.

7. Watch Time: This measures the total time viewers actually spend watching your video. Longer watch times suggest that your content is captivating and holds viewers' attention, which is favored by TikTok's algorithm.

8. Completion Rate: The percentage of viewers who watch your video from start to finish. A high completion rate suggests that your content is compelling and retains viewer interest throughout.

9. Click-Through Rate (CTR): If your video includes a call-to-action, CTR measures how many viewers take that action, such as visiting a website or clicking a link. This metric is crucial for driving traffic and conversions.

10. Hashtag Performance: Monitoring how well your hashtags perform reveals which tags enhance your visibility and engagement. Popular and relevant hashtags can expand your content's reach.

Regularly monitoring these metrics provides deeper insights into your content's performance, enabling data-driven decisions to optimize your TikTok strategy. This approach helps in creating more engaging content, growing your audience, and achieving your marketing objectives.

Tools and Techniques for Analyzing Performance

Analyzing the effectiveness of your TikTok campaigns is crucial for determining successful strategies. Here are effective methods and tools to assess and enhance your content's impact:

1. TikTok Analytics: TikTok offers an integrated analytics tool providing a comprehensive overview of your account's performance. It tracks metrics such as views, likes, comments, shares, follower growth, and more, offering insights into individual video performance and overall trends.

2. Google Analytics: For TikTok content directing traffic to your website, Google Analytics tracks visitor behavior, including the number of visitors from TikTok, their page visits, and session durations. This helps gauge the effectiveness of TikTok campaigns in driving website traffic and conversions.

3. Social Media Dashboards: Platforms like Hootsuite, Sprout Social, and Buffer consolidate data from various social media platforms, including TikTok. They aid in managing social media presence, scheduling posts, and analyzing performance across channels.

4. Hashtag Tracking Tools: Tools like Hashtagify and RiteTag analyze hashtag performance, highlighting trends and effectiveness. Optimizing hashtag strategies based on these insights can boost content visibility.

5. Engagement Analysis: Utilize TikTok Analytics to analyze engagement metrics like likes, comments, shares, and completion rates. Identify high-engagement videos and discern common factors contributing to their success.

6. Competitor Analysis: Monitor competitors' TikTok accounts to observe content types, audience engagement, and successful campaigns. This provides insights and inspiration for refining your own content strategy.

7. Surveys and Feedback: Directly gather qualitative insights from your audience through surveys and feedback. Understanding preferences alongside quantitative data enhances content strategy clarity.

8. A/B Testing: Experiment with diverse content types, posting times, and formats to evaluate

performance variations. Comparing results helps optimize strategies for improved outcomes.

By employing these tools and techniques, you can deepen your understanding of TikTok performance. Data-driven insights empower informed decisions, fostering more engaging content, broader audience reach, and effective achievement of marketing goals.

Iterating Based on Data and Feedback

Adapting your TikTok strategy using data and feedback is crucial for continual enhancement and maximizing effectiveness. Here's how to effectively utilize insights to refine your approach:

1. Analyze Performance Metrics: Regularly examine your TikTok Analytics and relevant data to detect trends and patterns in your content's performance. Focus on videos with high engagement rates, strong viewer retention, and significant shares, as

these indicate successful content that resonates well.

2. Identify Key Success Factors: Determine what aspects contribute to the success of your top-performing videos. Is it the content format, storytelling style, trending hashtags, or posting timing? Identifying these factors allows you to replicate them in future content, increasing your chances of success.

3. Address Areas Needing Improvement: Learn from videos that underperform by analyzing possible reasons for their lack of engagement. It could be due to mismatched audience preferences, unclear messaging, or ineffective calls-to-action. Use this feedback to adjust your content strategy accordingly.

4. Experiment and Test: Utilize A/B testing to experiment with different variables like video length, editing techniques, music choices, and CTAs. Compare the performance of various content versions to determine what resonates best

with your audience. Iterative testing helps refine your approach based on real data.

5. Incorporate Audience Input: Pay attention to audience comments, direct messages, and survey responses for valuable insights into their preferences and interests. Engage with your audience and integrate their feedback into your content strategy.

6. Remain Agile: TikTok trends and audience preferences evolve quickly. Stay flexible and responsive by adjusting your content strategy accordingly. Monitor emerging trends, adapt your content to capitalize on them, and stay ahead of the curve.

7. Measure Impact: Assess the effects of strategy adjustments on key metrics such as engagement levels, follower growth, and conversion rates. Understanding the impact helps identify the most effective strategies for achieving your objectives.

By continually refining your TikTok strategy based on data and feedback, you can optimize content performance over time, staying relevant and enhancing engagement with your audience. This iterative approach fosters ongoing improvement and strengthens your ability to achieve sustained success on TikTok.

Scaling Your TikTok Strategy for Long-term Success

Expanding your TikTok strategy involves broadening your reach, increasing engagement, and maintaining growth over time. Here's how to effectively scale your strategy:

1. Build on Successful Campaigns: Identify your top-performing TikTok campaigns and integrate their elements into future content. This may involve replicating content formats, employing similar storytelling methods, or collaborating with influencers who have previously delivered strong outcomes.

2. Diversify Content: Keep your content dynamic and varied to sustain audience interest. Experiment with diverse content types like tutorials, behind-the-scenes peeks, user-generated content, and trending videos. Diversifying content attracts a

broader audience and keeps your brand contemporary.

3. Expand Influencer Relationships: Cultivate solid partnerships with influencers who resonate with your brand ethos and possess a loyal following. Engage in multiple campaigns to establish familiarity and credibility with their audience, fostering sustained engagement and expansion.

4. Invest in Community Engagement: Interact actively with your TikTok community by responding to comments, hosting Q&A sessions, and showcasing user-generated content. Building community cultivates loyalty and encourages followers to advocate for your brand.

5. Monitor Trends and Adapt: Stay abreast of TikTok trends, algorithm updates, and shifts in audience preferences. Adjust your content strategy accordingly to capitalize on emerging trends and maintain visibility in the platform's dynamic landscape.

6. Optimize Content Discovery: Utilize trending hashtags, participate in challenges, and collaborate with influencers to enhance your content's discoverability. TikTok's algorithm favors engagement and relevance, so optimizing for discovery can amplify organic reach.

7. Measure Impact and Adapt: Continuously track key metrics such as engagement rates, follower growth, and campaign ROI. Use analytics tools to evaluate performance and make informed decisions on resource allocation, refining your strategy for maximum effectiveness.

8. Encourage Innovation: Foster creativity and innovation within your team or influencer network. Experiment with fresh content formats, storytelling techniques, or interactive features that set your brand apart and capture attention in TikTok's competitive environment.

By scaling your TikTok strategy strategically and consistently, you can achieve sustained success by reaching a wider audience, enhancing engagement, and driving continual growth for your brand on the platform.

Conclusion

Throughout this book, we've explored how TikTok serves as a potent platform for fashion brands aiming to excel in viral marketing and bolster their online presence. From grasping TikTok's audience and demographics to crafting compelling content and harnessing influencer collaborations, each chapter has offered practical strategies for navigating and thriving in the dynamic realm of social media marketing.

TikTok's distinctive blend of short-form videos, trends, and interactive features presents unparalleled opportunities for fashion brands to establish personal connections with consumers. By leveraging the platform's capabilities and staying attuned to trends, brands can cultivate a unique voice and cultivate a devoted following among TikTok's diverse user base.

Effective TikTok marketing transcends mere viral moments; it revolves around fostering authentic engagement and forging meaningful relationships with your audience. Whether through storytelling, educational content, or behind-the-scenes glimpses, brands can captivate viewers and inspire them to advocate for their products.

As you implement the strategies outlined in this book, keep in mind the importance of creativity, authenticity, and adaptability. TikTok is in a constant state of evolution, and successful brands are those that embrace change, experiment with new concepts, and continually refine their approach based on insights gleaned from data and feedback.

By setting clear objectives, monitoring performance metrics, and remaining informed about industry trends, fashion brands can position themselves for sustained success on TikTok. The journey to effective selling on TikTok demands commitment, strategic planning, and a profound understanding of your audience's preferences and behaviors.

As you embark on your TikTok marketing journey, remember that each interaction presents an opportunity to leave a lasting impression. Through consistent delivery of value, fostering community engagement, and staying true to your brand's essence, you can effectively market on TikTok and propel your fashion brand to new heights of achievement in the digital era.

www.ingramcontent.com/pod-product-compliance
Lightning Source LLC
LaVergne TN
LVHW051540050326
832903LV00033B/4357